Special Offer for You

Secure the Spy & Survival Bundle – a $497 Value – For FREE!

The Spy & Survival Bundle is our most sought after training and includes 7 modules such as evasive driving and the complete Escape & Evasion Survival System (a bug out bag on steroids.)

Available for a limited time at the website below!

www.FreeSp

1

Published by Spy Briefing, LLC
124 S. Main Street #4090
Cedar City, Utah 84720

Important Publishers Note

This publication is designed to provide accurate and authoritative information in regard to the subject matter covered. If legal advice or any type of assistance is needed, please seek the services of a competent professional. This book, published by the Spy Briefing, LLC, is for informational purposes only. All technical information, instruction, and advice, reflect the beliefs of Spy Briefing, LLC and are intended as informational only. This book is not intended to serve as a replacement for professional instruction. You agree to indemnify, and hold harmless the Spy Briefing, LLC and Jason R. Hanson from any and all such claims and damages as a result of reading this book, which is for informational purposes only.

Table of Contents

Introduction

Hi, I'm Chuck Masters.

Up until recently, I was a soybean-munching, latte-sipping, "no violence ever!" kind of guy.

But when I saw, with my own eyes…

… How a WW2 vet was harassed and assaulted while having dinner by a rabid ANTIFA and BLM mob…

… How ordinary Americans are bullied, robbed and attacked – daily – by vile thugs who are often hopped up on drugs…

… Stood face to face with a robber at knifepoint, realizing I had no clue what to do…

… My wife was crying over the phone because she barely escaped an attacker (probably a rapist) one night in a parking garage several thousand miles away…

And I was completely powerless to do anything. Something snapped in me.

Rage came over me and I had enough.

I was given the gift of desperation.

And set out to learn everything I could about how to defend myself and protect those I love – even strangers – when violence comes knocking.

Because rest assured violence is close by daily. Evil prowls around like a roaring lion, seeking someone to devour.

I've been assigned a duty – to learn and to teach you self-defense against evil.

I'll show you everything you need to know and do so that you can live in peace.

But I'll only share stuff that actually works in real-life, and that "normal folks" like you and I can do when our lives are on the line.

Tactic #1:
Palm Strikes

Real Life Scenario: 6-time Felon Knocked Cold In Brawl With 73-year-old During Attempted Home Invasion.

The man saw the men breaking into the back of his home, in the middle of the day, at which time he feared for his safety.

But, after hiding, anger kicked in and he mustered enough courage to attack.

They broke in, started searching for valuables, and without fear the man attacked the burglars with palm strikes.

Thanks to the element of surprise and the pain inflicted, the burglars fled the scene.

Purpose of a Palm Strike: Hitting someone with your fist isn't the most effective way to defend yourself.

Using the heel of your palm, instead of your balled up hand creates a wider, stronger strike.

It also reduces the risk of injury to yourself while inflicting more damage to your opponent.

Execute a Palm Strike

The palm strike uses the bottom inner portion of your hand to inflict maximum damage (when it connects to a vulnerable part of the body).

To execute a palm strike:

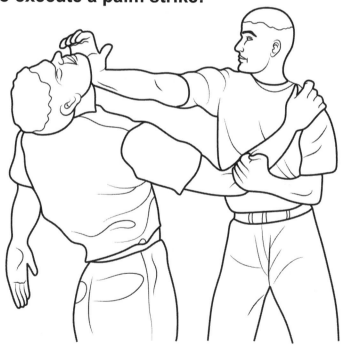

- Straighten out your fingers and thumb, as if you are about to give a salute.

- Bend your hand up and back until your hand is about 90 degrees from your arm, aligning the wrist.

- At this point, you may optionally choose to let your fingers relax, loosely bending at the knuckles.

Once your dominant hand is prepared to strike, it's important to understand the vulnerabilities of potential assailants.

Three of the weakest and most open points are:

- Chin: Often referred to as a "chin jab," simply take your prepared hand and thrust up into the face of your opponent, striking them just under the chin.

- Nose: A few inches above the chin, ramming your palm directly up and into the nose. This, perhaps, has the most potential lethality.

- Collarbone: If your attacker is somehow guarding the face, both collarbones will be exposed. This is a fairly weak, painful spot on the body. If struck with your aligned palm, it's likely to break.

Tactic #2:
Hammer Fists

Real Life Scenario No. 1: Cowboy, 79, Disarms Gunman with "Choke Fist Strike" To Throat.

A gunman carrying a rifle tried to break into a man's home. The man normally keeps a rifle next to his bed for coyotes, but didn't want to shoot the intruder. He chose to chop him in the neck instead.

When he saw the gunman and listened to his almost unintelligible gibberish, he decided to handle things differently.

"I didn't know whether to be scared or feel sorry for him," he said.

So, he hit the guy. Hard. Right in the throat.

"I just took that old hand and give him a good old chop," he said. "And normally, that really hurts bad."

Real Life Scenario No. 2: 58-Year-Old Woman Fights Off Rapist With a Pen & Punch.

This story proves that you don't need formal training to defend yourself, just the natural instinct to survive.

A 58-year-old woman was praying in a chapel when a male suspect attempted to force himself on her allegedly to rape her.

She had been taking notes in a journal with a pen, and when the man started to assault her, she channeled her inner Jason Bourne and stabbed the man several times in the neck with her pen. He quickly retreated.

Even though she was no professional MMA fighter, the woman had two very important skills: a survivor's instinct, ingenuity for turning common objects into weapons – and using a proper hammer punch or fist.

Never forget that just about anything can be used to strike an attacker. If you want to see my favorite improvised weapon and the one that I carry and use every day, check out www.TacticalSpyPen.com.

Purpose of Hammer Fists: Hammer fists, like palm strikes, focus on mitigating the risk of injury while maximizing the potential for damage.

A big, connected hit from the bottom of your fists (as opposed to your fingers) likely provides an opportunity to escape.

Execute a Hammer Fist

A traditional fist is where you ball up your fingers (thumb on the outside) and hurl it forward, fingers in front.

It's also one of the least effective strikes, for self defense — especially for someone who's not trained to fight.

That said, the same fist using the bottom portion of your hand, like a hammer, is incredibly effective.

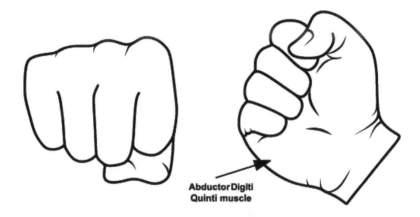

Abductor Digiti Quinti muscle

To execute a hammer fist:

- Make a fist by balling up all of your fingers, fairly tight.

- Remember to keep your thumb on the outside of your fist, wrapped in front of your knuckles.

- Move to strike with the bottom of your fist, like a hammer, not with the broadside of your fingers.

- For improved momentum, swing your hammer fist from the side, instead of straight forward (like a tomahawk).

Where to land a hammer fist:

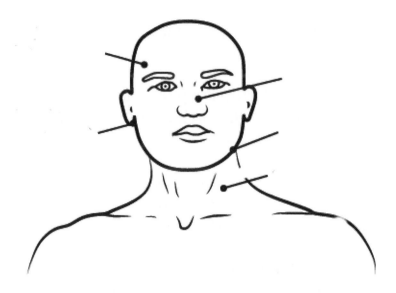

The hammer fist isn't for the front of the body. It's best executed on the side of the opponent's head. An exception to this is the nose, but that's often a better-protected location.

Other locations include:

- Slightly above and over from the eye.

- Directly below the ear.

- At the side bottom of the chin.

Tactic #3:
Elbow Strikes

Real Life Scenario: Man Fights Off Robbers, Douses Attackers From Gas Pump.

When three thugs encircled one man at the gas pump, he relied on this to knock two of them out – and then used the gas pump as a weapon to squirt gas on the attackers.

The wild incident begins with a man pumping gas by himself at night. It's a common situation, one we all find ourselves in frequently.

But then a van pulls up, and three passengers jump out. They immediately begin aggressively encircling the man. The suspects outnumber the man on the ground three to one, not counting the getaway driver.

Surely most folks would roll over here. While it's certainly OK to give up your wallet and cash, you can never truly know if an attacker means you further harm.

Keeping that in mind, this guy decides to fight back. Showing remarkable poise in the moment, he improvises, starts using the elbow strike first and then uses the gas pump as a weapon.

One-by-one, suspects attempt to corner the man around the opposite side of the vehicle. But head on a swivel, the man just keeps elbowing and dousing each attacker with fuel.

The attackers quickly get the message, abandoning their pursuit of the man.

Purpose of Elbow Strikes: Elbow blows provide the largest attack area, by using the forearm to strike opponents.

This creates less opportunity for error, and often more force.

Execute an Elbow Strike

Using your forearm and elbow creates a larger surface area while also bringing in more momentum from your body.

You're not trying to throw a punch with your arm and hand, but attacking with the power of most of your body.

To execute an elbow strike:

- Bend your dominant arm, at the elbow.

- Bring your hand to the center of your chest.

- Step into your opponent with your opposite leg (if you're right-handed, step in with your left).

- Strike with the lower half of your forearm, broadside into your target.

Where to land an elbow strike:

- Throat: The throat is the easiest target. With the thrust of your whole body going into your forearm, it's likely you'll connect given an opportunity.

- Side of the head: The temple area, above the eye, and the jawline are perfect targets. Land your elbow strike there and it'll likely create an escape opening.

- Kidney or Groin: Sometimes the chance to defend yourself comes after you're caught. If you're on your knees, the best alternative is to try and elbow strike the kidney, or even groin area, depending on height.

- At the side bottom of the chin.

Tactic #4:
Power Slaps

Real Life Scenario: Carjacking Victim Smacks Away Gun, Slams Attacker.

After a thug stuck a gun in a man's face outside his home, the carjacking victim fought back and violently slammed his attacker.

A home surveillance video caught the wild scene in California. A couple of thugs attempted to carjack a man outside his home.

But even at gunpoint, this guy was having none of it. The carjacking victim smacked the gun out of the suspect's hands and violently body slammed him, ending the threat.

Police said suspects approached the victim with a gun. With the footage caught on tape by a nearby security camera, the victim appears to parry the gun away from his face. He then picks up and violently slams one of the suspects.

More importantly, the incident illustrates the need to maintain constant situational awareness. Though the thugs seemingly got the drop on the man, he managed to quickly turn the tables.

He found his opening, and then emphatically and violently, exploited that opening.

Purpose of Power Slaps: Slapping isn't something many reference when discussing self-defense.

But by using the lower part of your inner hand, in the right location, it's devastating.

Execute a Power Slap

Slapping is often seen as a way to insult or sting someone, rather than a defense tactic.

But a properly executed power slap renders attackers dazed and confused.

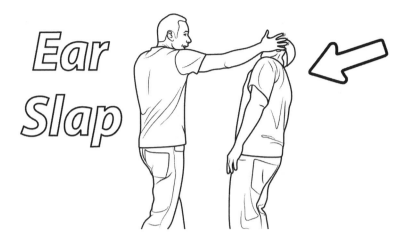

To execute a power slap:

- Hit with your lower palm, not fingers:
  Like a palm strike, your goal is to use
  the lower part of your hand. Fingers
  won't do the damage you need to
  defend yourself. When you hit, make
  sure it's the bottom half of your open
  hand.

- Aim through your target: Some slap to
  sting others while not feeling it
  themselves. You want your target to be
  injured or temporarily unable to attack.
  For that, aim all the way through. For
  instance, if you want to hit the right ear,
  use the amount of force it takes to get to
  the left side of their head. Convince

yourself of this and you'll hit much harder.

- Practice your aim: This is one of the most precision strikes on the list. Others use powerful strikes or broad surface areas. This one is a bit smaller and must connect to a vulnerable place on the body. Practice makes perfect.

Where to land a power slap:

- Ear: Slapping directly flat on the ear is effective (both is even more effective, but not a likely scenario unless you're fully behind your opponent)

- Back of the jaw: Right where the jawbone connects to the head is vulnerable and susceptible to a slap. If you connect, it's likely an attacker will instantly feel he's injured.

- Eye: If your capture/opponent becomes distracted and looks to the left or right, a solid slap to the eye is brutal. Connect straight on, like the ear, if possible.

Tactic #5:
Short Range Punches

Real Life Scenario: 82-Year-Old Vietnam Vet Beats Armed Intruder to Death With Shotgun Butt.

When a suspect with a knife allegedly broke in and attacked his wife, 82-year-old Herb A. went to work.

There's tough, there's "old man tough," and then there's surviving Vietnam only to punch a knife attacker to death at 82 years old tough.

Herb, a Vietnam Vet from South Carolina, proved exactly that tough when he fought off and killed a knife-wielding home intruder.

The incident began when a man knocked on the door of Herb and his 79-year-old wife, Lois, according to reports.

The couple said the man asked about a dog, before things turned deadly.

"I opened the door and he said he was looking for his little white chihuahua and wanted to know if I saw it," he said. "I told him no, I hadn't."

That's when the suspect, a 61-year-old, forced his way inside. Armed with a knife, he allegedly used the handle of the weapon to hit the couple. Herb suffered a cut to his forehead, according to multiple reports.

"I felt, we're done. He's going to kill us and take what he can take," Herb said. "He was not going to go out that door and leave us alive. That's the way I felt. That's why I said, 'I've got to do something quick and get the edge on him. Get the advantage on him.'"

Herb decided to fight. He charged the attacker and proceeded to punch his attacker to death. Now that's some Ho Chi Minh level close combat.

One neighbor says: "This street is normally not that crazy or anything and we all know each other. I never would have expected it to happen here. I kinda feel like it puts a stain on this neighborhood in a way."

"But when I heard they were able to fend off the suspect, I was so proud of them and I was like, 'OK, so that guy picked the wrong house.'"

Purpose of Short-Range Punches: If your attacker is too close, a big strike is out of the question.

For this scenario, you need the ability to punch powerfully at close range.

Execute Short Range Punches

Short-range punches are more about form and target than power.

That said, it doesn't hurt to practice on a punching bag and lift weights to increase muscle in the arms.

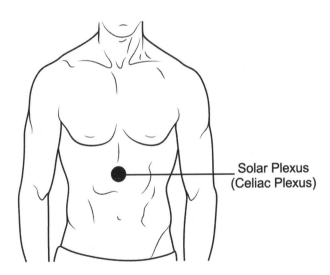

Solar Plexus
(Celiac Plexus)

To execute a short-range punch:

- Ball up a traditional fist.

- Focus on connecting with the knuckle on your middle finger (often the most pronounced).

- If possible, strike coming up or down, not straight on to generate as much force possible.

Where to land a short-range punch:

Again, you're in tight quarters. Perhaps the attacker has grabbed you and you manage to push back enough to get in one strike before they pull you back into their grasp.

This situation, and similar ones, are where this strike is useful. But only if you understand vulnerabilities to target.

- Solar plexus: This little spot is right at the bottom of the sternum, a couple inches above where the common belly button rests. Get a decent-enough amount of force here and the fight is likely over.

- Nose: In the scenario where you're pulling away, the attacker is likely concentrated on pulling and grabbing, not protecting their nose. Pop them and they may even let go entirely.
- Throat: Likewise scenario, if they're concentrated on subduing you, they'll not be ready for a punch to the throat.

Tactic #6:
Knee Strikes

Real Life Scenario No. 1: How One 67-year-old Homeowner Fights Like Hell, Pummels Armed Intruders Using His "Bad Knee".

When two armed intruders posed as police responding to the COVID-19 pandemic, a Chicago homeowner fought back, pummeling the bad guys.

Two burglars picked a fight they couldn't win, leaving one in jail and the other dead.

Police say the two armed intruders entered a private residence after tricking their way inside. Then they attempted to rob a couple at gunpoint. The suspects targeted the home specifically, according to police.

The suspects planned the robbery to match Illinois' stay-at-home order in response to COVID-19. Footage shows the two men arriving at the front door wearing PPE masks and gloves.

The two men tricked their way inside the house, occupied by a 50-year-old man, his 48-year-old wife and their two kids, ages 14 and

11. Police say they carried a bag containing zip ties and a blow torch.

When the two men pulled weapons, a massive fight followed, as the homeowner engaged the intruders with knee strikes.

Footage shows the fight spill back outside in front of the house, where the homeowner pummels the intruders unconscious with knee strikes and then punches.

He fought like hell to protect his family, and the good guy came out a winner in the end.

Real Life Scenario No. 2: Texas Mom Lays Out Alleged Peeper With Bone-Crushing Knee Strike

A Texas mom kneed and tackled a suspected peeper, a man who had recently been caught looking through her daughter's window.

The suspect promptly evaded two officers. But the mother laid a nice hit on the perp, bringing him down until police were able to make the arrest.

"I figured it's the least I could do, if I got him down, tripped him up, whatever, then they would have the chance to get caught up," she says. "First instinct was just to make sure he didn't go any further."

With her daughter looking on, footage shows the mom taking matters into her own hands. She rushes in without hesitation, risking personal injury.

The mother's actions proved heroic. But her courage to act came from a place typically reserved for parents.

"My kids are my life, and I was just making sure I protected them," she said.

Purpose of Knee Strikes: Oftentimes, an attacker grabs you.

At this moment, you only have a few options.

Knee strikes allow you to deliver a powerful strike into a couple of vulnerable areas of the body.

Execute a Knee Strike

The knee is a powerful weapon, when used properly.

It's bigger than your hand, even your arms, and is likely stronger.

However, it can take more coordination, as you may want to pull your attacker down into your strike.

To execute a knee strike:

- Step back with your dominant leg, or move your other leg forward.

- Switch your weight to the leg in front of you.

- Bring up your dominant leg, hiking up the knee into your target with as much force as you can muster.

- Optional: If possible, grab your opponent and pull them closer or even into your strike, for maximum damage.

Where to land knee strike:

- Groin: The groin is a target virtually anyone can reach with their knee. If the attacker winds up too close for comfort and directly in front of you, knee them right between the legs.

- Solar plexus: If the attacker has grabbed you from a lower center of gravity, the groin is protected and the face is too far away. If you have a free leg drive the knee into their solar plexus, at the bottom of the sternum.

- Face: Say the opponent makes a mistake, throws a punch and you dodge it. While recovering from the missed punch, grab them with your hands at the same time you're moving the knee upwards. Pull their head straight into the knee.

Tactic #7:
Groin Kick

Real Life Scenario: Colorado Woman Thwarts Bathroom Attacker with "Belt Buckle Squeeze".

She told deputies when she walked into the restroom, the man had been hiding behind the door.

He attacked her with a knife and knocked her to the ground, trying to keep her inside.

The woman said during the struggle she was able to use the "Belt Buckle Squeeze" causing him to fall backward, allowing her to escape and lock herself inside the bathroom until help arrived.

The groin kick in this chapter shows you how to do this with your leg and feet, but you can just as easily use it with your hands to inflict a tremendous amount of pain.

Purpose of Groin Kicks: A swift kick to this vital area, especially for men, will take attackers down and leave them in pain for hours, or even days.

Plus, the power of your leg makes it hard to block, even when using hands and arms.

Execute a Groin Kick

See an oncoming attacker?

Act like you don't notice or get in some sort of weak, submissive stance (i.e. fake panic with both of your arms up toward them).

And when they come in range of your boot, give it to them where it hurts.

To execute a groin kick:

- Wait for the right moment, if the person sees it coming, groin kicks are easy to defend.

- Step forward with your off leg (your dominant kicking leg back).

- Immediately swing that dominant leg to its target, full speed ahead

Targeting the groin area:

Obviously, a groin kick is a single target area. But you're not going for a quick tap, like a college dorm prank.

This is a life-or-death scenario and you want to come out on top, or at least with a decent chance to escape.

Tip: Convince yourself you'll kick well into his belly button, it'll help you achieve more force. This isn't to see him grab his privates and fall, like in a viral video. You want him to be incapacitated.

Tactic #8:
Leg Kicks

Purpose of Leg Kicks: Most untrained attackers protect their upper body, leaving their legs vulnerable.

Some of the open spots are excruciating and fairly easy to strike, for self-defense beginners.

Execute Leg Kicks

Except for the groin kick, leg kicks for self-defense look different than many imagine.

You're not doing spins, or kicking bamboo like in a movie.

In fact, some of the easiest kicks for self-defense are more like stomps.

Figure 5-5. Shin kick to legs.

To execute a leg kick:

- Choose the target, depending on how you and your opponent are standing.

- Raise your leg as high as you can, without losing your balance.

- Come down as hard as possible, not caring if it snaps the person's bone, but even trying to do it.

Where to land a leg kick:

It's based on availability. If the attacker came from behind, the shin or inner lower leg would work. If they're shorter than you, a solid strike to the knee would be excruciating.

- Shin: If the shin is the most open, don't just lift your heel to kick. Bring up the leg and come down at about a 45-degree angle as hard as you can muster.

- Inner lower leg: When entangled, see if your opponent is in a wide stance. The inner leg, about 4-6 inches above the ankle is one of the most powerful pressure points on the body. Kick here with no mercy.

- Knee: If you practice a side or front kick (meaning you kick with the bottom of your foot forward) the knee is a great target. Stomp kicks are much better for beginners and lower legs are more vulnerable.

Tactic #9:
Rear Choke

Purpose of Rear Choke: If the opportunity presents itself, a choke incapacitates your attacker without causing a lot of noise.

If you're in a kidnapping situation and find yourself with one guard, it could be the best way to escape without alerting others.

Execute a Rear Choke

There are two primary methods for choking someone

- One where your forearm and bicep are on either side of the neck (This is called a "rear naked choke").

- Another where you use your forearm to dig deep into the front of the neck.

Completely locking your arm around the neck is more effective. There are two points, one on either side of the neck, that render a person unconscious faster than if you were simply pushing up/pulling back on the center of the throat.

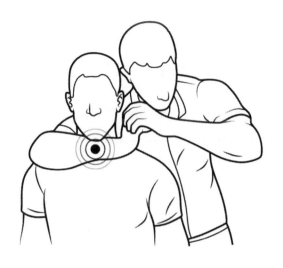

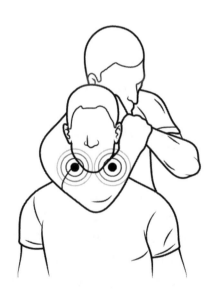

To execute a rear choke:

- Wait for the right moment and only when there is one attacker (others will come to help and you'll be vulnerable).

- Ensure you can get your arm around them and clench before they notice.

- Wrap your entire arm around their neck, with your bicep digging into one side and your forearm digging into the other.

- Place your other arm behind their head grabbing the shoulder of the arm around their neck.

- Push forward with the arm behind their head as you pull back with the arm around their neck.

- Hold on for a few seconds after they are on the ground passed out.

Tactic #10:
Eye Rake/Gouge

Real Life Scenario: A 70-year-old Man Laid A Beating On An Intruder Who Smashed Through A Window In His Home.

He heard loud banging outside his home at about 3 a.m. on a Saturday, and at first, thought it was a bear. But when he got up to look outside he didn't see anything.

He then looked in front of his home and saw a man falling over trash barrels. He went to call the police and when he turned around the man was inside the house.

The 70-year-old says the man smashed through a window and entered through his breezeway.

He grabbed the intruder, and hit him three times with the Eye Rake and Gouge move.

He says he used the braces he wears on his arms for arthritis like boxing gloves.

Purpose of an Eye Rake or Gouge: Eyes are incredibly sensitive and vulnerable.

If an attacker can't see you, it's highly unlikely they'll be able to follow you.

Take out one eye (or both) and you'll no longer be their priority.

Execute an Eye Rake

Sometimes a strike isn't possible.

Your attacker comes too close, too quickly and you just can't kick or punch.

Many times, you're grabbed from behind.

It's in these situations that an eye gouge or eye rake is ideal.

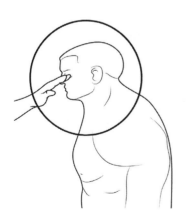 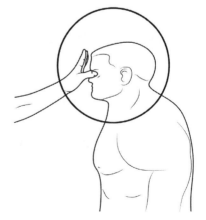

There are a few reasons for this:

- You can execute with an attacker in front of you and behind you.

- The assailants focus will change from grabbing you to protecting their vulnerable eyes.

- If you successfully take out an eye, it will be much easier to escape or get out of their grasp.

To execute an eye rake:

- Get or keep at least one arm free.

- Move your hand quickly to the head, where the eyes are likely to be (if you can't see).

- Dig, scratch, grab and pull.

- It's important not to show mercy. It's better for your attacker to permanently lose an eye than for you to be beaten, kidnapped or worse.

Important note for eye rake/gouge:

This is an instinctual move that you can practice. If you're in a situation where this is your best move, you'll be glad you practiced this.

Get someone to help you by pretending to grab you from behind, or put you in a (loose) choke position.

Then, practice raising your hand to the eye level. (Make sure you and your partner aren't hurting one another. Safety goggles are a good starting point.)

Tactic #11:
Back Fist Strike

Real Life Scenario: Petite Woman, 68, Pulls Granddaughter From Hands Of Intruder.

A woman was in her kitchen when she heard the front door open and heard her granddaughter screaming.

A man grabbed the toddler from inside the home by way of an unlocked front door.

But the woman pried the kid free and landed several blows that knocked out the attacker long enough for the police to show up to the scene.

Purpose of a Back Fist Strike: A back fist isn't a traditional strike, leaving many opponents vulnerable to it, because they're not looking for it and don't see it coming.

Execute a Back Fist Strike

Make a fist and hold it out in front of you, with the forearm down (almost like you're a superhero flying).

You'll probably notice the two knuckles of your index and middle fingers stick up a bit higher than the rest.

In a back fist strike, it's those two knuckles you're trying to land in a vulnerable area of your opponent.

The best time for this is when you're bent toward one side of your attacker.

For example, if they had a knife and you swatted their arm to one side, and clawed away until the knife was out of their hand.

The next step (after kicking the knife away) would be to strike the attacker.

Since your weight is to one side of them, using the back of your fist to strike is a useful tactic.

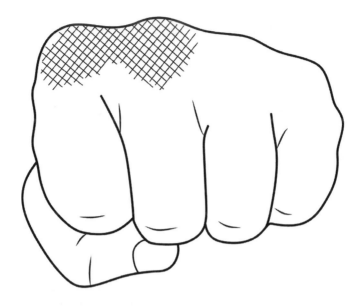

To execute a back fist strike:

- Clench a normal fist (with the thumb on the outside).

- Take a step toward your opponent with the leg of the same side of the arm with which you plan to strike (or to the opposite side, if you're to one side of them).

- Swing from your shoulder down to the back of your forearm with the endgame to hit a vulnerable area with the knuckles on the back of your fist—as hard as you possibly can.

Areas to target include:

- Temple

- Throat

- Eyes

- Groin (if you're down on the ground and that's closest)

Tactic #12:
Liver Punch

Real Life Scenario: 72-Year-Old Retired Boxer Pummels Burglar With These Three Simple Moves.

A burglar broke into a man's home and threatened him with a knife. The man dodged the knife and ran through a series of strikes that knocked him out.

A retired boxer defended his home when a burglar broke in and threatened him with a knife, but got more than he bargained for.

The boxer, who served with the Royal Engineers in North Africa from 1956-1958, dodged the knife and punched the attacker twice in the face, giving him a black eye and a swollen lip – and then used a liver punch to finish him off.

He then restrained the attacker until police arrived.

Purpose of a Liver Punch: The liver is sometimes referred to as the "second brain," due to its numerous functions and how vital it is for life.

Connect with the liver well enough and your attacker won't be focused on the fight.

Execute a Liver Punch

A liver punch is more of a traditional boxing or street fighting punch.

It wouldn't be ideal if your opponent was much bigger, or hardened.

Bottomline: If it looks like they can take a punch and you're not able to deliver one powerfully—Look for another strike.

However, if you've been practicing and know you can throw a good punch, on target, the liver is a potential fight-ender.

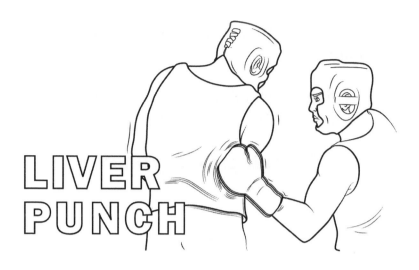

LIVER PUNCH

To execute a liver punch:

This is all about timing and the ability to throw a punch.

One example is that you're down on the ground and your attacker's back opens up.

Another would be that you've managed to pull their body down but can't manage a powerful knee strike.

In both scenarios (again, if you can generate the power) a liver punch is effective.

The liver is located on the back, right side underneath the bottom part of the ribcage. Ribs are bone, albeit fragile, so keep that in mind.

A few additional tactical notes:

- Ball up a traditional fist (thumb out).

- Try to twist your body back, at the hip on the side of your dominant hand (if you can do so).

- Move the hip in, followed by the shoulder and your hand as hard as you can into the target area.

- No mercy, try to break the ribs surrounding the liver.

- Practice on a punching dummy that looks like a man. Draw a fake liver with a marker, if you have to, for reference.

Tactic #13:
Reinforced Finger Poke

Purpose of Reinforced Finger Poke: Like a short-distance punch, just with your more fingers.

Since vulnerable areas, like the throat or eyes are small targets, sometimes it takes a finger poke.

Execute a Reinforced Finger Poke

The term "reinforced" in this case simply means more than one finger.

Don't go jabbing at someone's throat with a single digit.

Three, or even four works fine.

Most people don't have trouble extending their index, middle and ring fingers while folding the pinky, but it's a good idea to try first.

To execute a reinforced finger poke:

- Extend at least two fingers (index and middle fingers or index, middle and ring).

- Choose a target on your attacker.

- Jab hard, not to hit the surface, but drive your fingers deep into their body.

Areas vulnerable to a reinforced finger poke:

- Eyes: Jabbing at a single eye is probably the easiest target. Although, you could use four fingers, spreading them like Spock and going for your best Larry, Curly and Moe impression.

- Throat: The very center of the throat is incredibly vulnerable. Hit it, even with a reinforced finger poke, and the biggest opponent will be gasping for air.

.

Tactic #14:
Reverse Knife Hand Strike

Purpose of a Reverse Knife Hand Strike: A knife hand strike is known in pop culture as a "karate chop."

Using the opposite edge of your hand is another little-known strike that catches almost everyone off guard.

It's used for more vulnerable points, like the throat.

Execute a Reverse Knife Hand Strike

Self-defense is taking advantage of weaknesses or vulnerabilities.

That takes knowing how to use various parts of your body, in as many ways as possible.

The reverse knife hand is one of those tactics that most assailants would never see coming.

Note: This isn't going to be a good strike for a jaw or body, but striking right in the throat or upward into the groin will catch them off guard while rendering them unable to continue the fight.

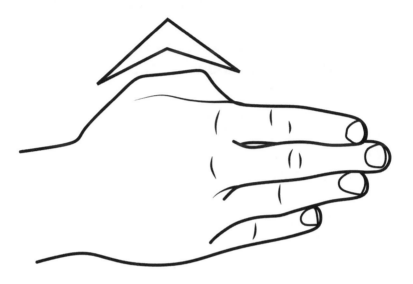

To execute a reverse knife hand strike:

- Make a "karate chop" hand by extending all of your fingers straight, including your thumb.

- Turn your whole body toward your opponent, including your arm hurling toward the target, thumb knuckle first.

- Attempt to strike directly on the front of the throat or directly up into the groin of your attacker.

- Again, strike like you don't want to stop at the target, but go straight through them

When to strike with a reverse knife hand:

- If the target is the throat, it's best if the attacker is to the side, so the full force hits them right in the trachea.

- If you're bent over low, the best move may be to uppercut (with your reverse knife hand) directly between the legs.

Again, this strike (and the others) are meant to help you have a tool bag, full of tactics.

That way, no matter how close or far your attacker hits—you have something to throw at them and defend yourself.

Bonus Chapter:
How to Escape and Evade a Mob (or Riot)

It seems like unrest pops up within minutes of breaking news nowadays, doesn't it? A protest quickly turns into a riot. Mobs gather to break and take what isn't theirs.

There's a world of difference between watching clips of angry rioters and actually being in their midst.

If you find yourself in the sights or in the middle of unrest, you need to escape — as soon as possible.

3 Tips to Escape, Evade and Survive

1. Keep Your Eye on the Situation (Before Unrest Occurs)

If you live in a large city, or urban area, there are multiple situations just waiting to heat things up. The better you understand your area and listen to the right places, you'll know when these things are (possibly) about to occur.

A few ways to keep your ear to the ground:

- Get a police scanner (or a scanner app): Some apps pool together people broadcasting their police scanners. You can even change settings to alert you when a certain number of people are listening to your area's police signal. Like a tornado warning, for trouble.

- Know hotspot areas: On your way to work, in the morning, are people gathering in popular places? If you see a protest sign at 9 a.m., others are likely to join later on.

- Have a plan: Not just a single escape route, but multiple ways out and even multiple potential places you may be. For instance, from work, the park, your friends/family's house.

2. In the Midst of a Mob or Riot

Look, sometimes the most prepared find themselves in the middle of tough situations. For that, you need situational awareness and a couple of good tactics to blend in:

- Change appearance: If possible, carry something like a hoodie around. Your suit or polo isn't going to cut it. No hoodie? Wear an undershirt and take off the polo.

- Find protest paraphernalia: Pick up a sign, move to the back of a mob. Oftentimes, those are there to protest, not to pick a fight. Once you're in the back, look for someone with supplies (handmade signs, buttons, pamphlets, etc.) Take what you can, including a bottle of water (common item handed out and it makes you look more natural and devoted to be there for the long haul).

- After you fit in, look for the best way out: Police tend to corral groups. The angrier mobs will confront them head on, but some officers may be at other points (side streets, etc.) You're dressed to not be a target of the mob, but make yourself a potential threat to police. Find an open street (and a trash can along the way). Discard some items after you're in the clear.

3. Be ready to Defend Yourself

It's absolutely best to avoid confrontation. You're there and don't know many people. The crowd came in groups. That means, others will quickly see you're alone and not really a part of their cause.

If you do find yourself in physical confrontation, it's best to try and end it quickly. For that, you'll need to know and practice a few moves:

- Palm strikes: Bend your hand back and strike with the open face bottom of your palm. It's brutal, but if your life is threatened, it packs a bigger punch than a fist.

- Vulnerable areas: The nose, throat, groin, collar bone. These areas stop assailants in their tracks.

- Elbow strikes: For a larger surface area, bend your arm and push the broadside of your elbow into an opponent's throat. It's useful for pushing the attacker into others, if you're being attacked by multiple people.

Bonus Chapter:
How to Defend Against Multiple Attackers

When you're not looking for a fight, even one person is too many. But imagine two, three or even four attackers — all at the same time.

There are a number of things you must do, because the odds are against you. Here's our list of things to remember:

8 Things to Know When Defending Against Multiple Attackers

- Escape if possible: Take a quick look for escape routes, these fights don't always happen in a dead-end alley. If you're fast, it's a good idea to try and escape the trouble.

- Use your words: Nowhere to run? Try and talk your way out of it. Don't spit, snarl and curse. Explain yourself, calmly shielding them from seeing fear. Apologize, even if it's not your fault. (Sometimes, you can try and talk your way out while looking for an escape route.)

- Look for leverage (a weapon): Another thing to possibly do, while talking, look for something to use as a weapon. Tree limb, trash can lid (or the can), rocks. Pick it up quickly, this will be your next move if your negotiations fail.

- Watch them closely (before they attack): Who's the leader? Is one of them unsure about this? Who's in front, likely to attack first? Does it seem premeditated? All important things to assess. If anything, it helps you keep your head in the game.

- Strike one hard, fast and brutal: Nothing's working and one is headed right for you. He's in an alpha state of mind, you're putting off the calm feeling. It's likely he won't expect a practiced, no mercy strike from you. Hands aren't up? Palm strike him right in the nose. He'll drop and the others will think twice. Protecting his head? Kick downward on his inner leg, or knee. The scream will also shock his companions. Convince yourself not to care what happens to him and connect hard, trying to go through his skull or straight through the bone of his leg.

- If you think you can get away, run: Now's a chance to run, but if you're in that unfortunate dead-end alley, it's best to talk again and avoid conflict.

- If you can't get away, talk (again): Reiterate that you don't want trouble, that you're sorry. Now, add that you're prepared to defend yourself, but just want to go home.

- Be ready with different strikes: If the friends want to finish the job, or don't care about the guy who's on the ground. Know different and effective ways to strike. They'll probably be preparing to defend against what you just did.

Bonus Chapter:
How to Defend
Against a Carjacking

Real Life Scenario: Woman's Car Keys
Saved Her Life.

The mother of 6 remembered a self-defense tactic her mother taught her

A mother in Amarillo, Texas, has become a social media hero after fighting off an attacker one early morning.

She was punched in the nose by a man in the parking lot of her apartment complex at 2:30am after going out to her car to retrieve a phone charger.

Thankfully, her own mother had taught her a self-defense tactic years before: Carry your keys between your fingers.

So, she punched the man in the neck with a right hook, stabbing him with those keys, and he fled, holding his neck.

The woman then immediately went to the police to report the attack, and officers were able to collect the assailant's DNA from her keys.

Carjacking's happen frequently in larger cities. Sometimes, there are so many that local law enforcement doesn't really investigate them.

This unfortunate reality means it's up to you to ensure your vehicle (and your person) are as safe as possible.

How To: There are two primary ways to do this—Prevention and Defense.

Try everything possible to prevent a car theft/carjacking. And when necessary, know how to defend your belongings if you're in/at your vehicle when it's being jacked.

Steps to Prevent Carjacking

- Location, location, location: Where you park is important. If there is a parking garage that has security cameras, and even attendants, it's probably the best option. If not, try parking in a crowded area that's well lit. Obviously, if the area you're in isn't safe, the traffic level and amount of light won't matter. Ask yourself, where is the safest place to park where I'm headed? That should go a long way.

- Common sense measures: Think about what your parents would tell you to do. Lock your doors, make sure the windows are closed, and don't have any valuables clearly visible (Note: It's probably better to remove all valuables from the car. Some carjackers look for well-kept cars, knowing their owners may have something good in the glove compartment).

- Above and beyond measures: As mentioned, some of the biggest cities are so riddled with crime, cars are easy targets. Extreme times may call for extreme measures. For example, keep your car a bit on the dirty side (interior and exterior). This is ideal for a work car, you don't have friends in it, but take it to work deep in the city. If there is a shiny car, with the windows cracked, a thief will pass you up to go after better-looking prey.

Defend Against Carjacking

- Awareness: A carjacker is going to have tools. Whether it's a blunt object to bust your window, a screwdriver, or something else. They also may be professional criminals. Some are looking for valuables to sell, others are part of a group to take cars for parts. Try to understand who's coming at you. For instance, someone who looks high on drugs versus someone who's focused with a tool-in-hand.

- Talk first: The goal here is to get away, car or not. If it's a hardened pro, the best option may be to give up your keys. While they have a tool in their hand, a gun could be in their pants.

- Strike fast and hard: If talking isn't an option, like the assailant tells you to get in the car, don't act scared. But don't act like you're going to fight. Stay calm, but pick out a weak target to strike. Handling a tool, someone is less likely to be protecting their vulnerable areas. A surprise palm strike to the nose or a full force kick to the knee are likely to take them by surprise. After all, their mind is probably on getting out of there (with your car) without being caught.

Bonus Chapter:
How to Disarm an Attacker with a Knife or Gun

Disarming a knife-wielding attacker

- Try to get distance: A knife, as opposed to a gun, is all about keeping your distance as long as possible. A short blade can't hurt you if you're out of range. Plus, when the attacker comes at you, he'll likely telegraph how he's going to strike (either stab or slash). This knowledge gives you a bit more control over the situation.

- Focus on the weapon: The attacker, if they really intend to harm you, will be looking for a weak spot to strike. You should concentrate on the knife. It's highly unlikely the assailant would hold a knife just to punch you with their off hand.

- Use a shield (if possible): A trash can lid, tree limb, even a traffic cone. The closest carriable item to you with the largest surface area.

- Grab with both hands/arms and push the attacker down: Once the attacker lunges, the only thing you can do is dodge and attempt to grab that arm. Try to get a hand (of yours) as close to the hand/fist of the attacker as possible. Then, wrap your other arm closer to their upper arm/shoulder and push them down. They'll concentrate on staying on their feet, moving their attention away from handling the knife.

- Pry the knife away from them: Claw, pull and even bite (if you have to) to get that knife out of their hand. Remember: Once it's away, kick it away from them, they'll likely scramble to pick up the weapon.

- Strike while you can: Now it's time to make your getaway, but first you have to wound your attacker. If they're still bent over, it could be a perfect time to forcefully bring your knee right into their nose, temple or chin. Once they're injured, you have the opportunity to bolt.

Disarming a Gun-toting Attacker

- Do what they want (if you can): Most (certainly not all) people don't want to kill someone else. A gun is often to make theft easier, but it also makes death easier, too. You're seriously outmatched even if it's a novice with a gun (unless you're packing). If they ask for something, give it to them. Telegraph your moves. One example is to say something, "Ok, I'm slowly reaching for my wallet in my back pocket."

- Close the distance (carefully): This is the opposite of the knife. Handguns have an ideal range. It's not too far, but out of reach is also worse for you. If you're 4-5 feet away, anyone can hit vital areas. 2 feet makes aiming a bit more difficult (not much), but it also gives you the range to defend yourself. Don't move quickly. Take a half step as you reach for your wallet, making the move seem as natural as possible.

- From behind: An armed attacker coming from behind is tricky. They don't want you to see their face, so offering to give them what they want is a solid strategy. But if you don't have cash, it could incite a deadly incident. For that, quickly move your head, turn and strike vulnerable areas in one swift movement. An elbow strike is ideal, you'll have a larger surface area. With your other hand, grab the hand with the gun ensuring it's away from you.

- From the front: Frontal attacks are a bad deal (worse than the other bad deals). For this, after trying diplomatic solutions, close that distance (naturally). Then, move your body one way and swat/strike the armed hand the other way. Grab the wrist, closing the rest of the distance between you and the attacker. Grab the arm and push down, much like the knife scenario. Then, claw and grapple the gun away, strike and move.

Bonus Chapter:
How to Defend Yourself Against an (Armed) Robbery

There are really two elements to defending yourself against robbery.

One is active, meaning in the moment of being robbed. You're in the situation. A thief is there to take what you have.

The other defensive mechanism is passive, meaning you always anticipate the potential threat of robbery—trying as best you can to prevent it from actually happening.

You need both skills. One "just in case it happens," because even the best preparations won't thwart all harm.

The other, though, will likely keep you, your belongings and your family safer than the average person.

Passive Methods to Defend Against Robbery

- Situational Awareness: Skilled robbers often scope out their prey, knowing that the overwhelming majority of people don't look for threats. Don't be like most people, look for people who aren't there to have a good time. Look at the corners, dark spots and people alone. See if they're looking for someone, without wanting to be seen. Something fishy? React before a robbery occurs, by leaving or keeping your guard up.

- Numbers and Light: Groups and well-lit areas are the enemy of someone who professionally steals from others. When possible, travel and hang out in groups and stay in lit areas, close to the action. When you have to be alone, move quickly and stay out of potential corners/traps.

- Be Boring: In your day-to-day, it's more important to stay safe than flash fancy things to strangers. One of those strangers could want to take it. Do your best to dress, act and carry yourself like an average person. Robbers are looking for shiny, well-dressed folks.

Active Methods to Defend Against Robbery

- Situational Awareness: This is as needed with a robber standing in front of you as it is beforehand (more, actually). How do they carry themselves? Do they have a weapon? Is someone else with them, nearby? Is there a clear way out, to escape? Is there something I can use as a weapon? Think, keep your mind active and present.

- Calm is Better: The robber will act powerful, in control. Let them. Don't match their energy with aggression. Likewise, don't show fear. Both are likely to accelerate violence. Stay calm, be reasonable and submissive. Give them what they want and see if they leave.

- See an Opening and Strike (No Mercy): If it's more than a simple robbery, you must defend yourself to keep from being a victim (of trafficking, or worse). Switch your situational awareness to find a vulnerable spot. If they're attempting to grab you low, use that palm strike and send their nose into their face.

Bonus Chapter:
How to Defend Yourself with Canes, Walking Sticks and Umbrellas

Real Life Scenario No. 1: Teenager Whacks an Attacker Into submission with His Grandfather's Cane.

The grandkids were staying at their grandparents' home, when they were woken by a noise in the living room.

When one of the kids looked out of his room and didn't see anything, he went back to bed, but heard another noise a short time later.

"I looked out and saw someone in the living room, and the TV that was hanging on the wall was on the floor," he said in an interview. "I saw my grandfather's cane in the hallway, so I reached in and grabbed it and basically went after the guy with it, yelling at him to get out."

The teenager chased the intruder out of the house, striking him once in the back with the cane.

Real Life Scenario No. 2: "He Cried Like A Baby" – 81-year-old Woman Batters Intruder With Pair Of Crutches.

An intruder forced his way into an 81-year-olds home. He should've left this lady alone. She used a simple tactic to beat the crap out of him.

Although the thief managed to escape with $110 from the victim's purse, he was forced to flee after she used her crutches to hit him around the head.

How To: I highly recommend training to use a cane, walking stick, crutch, or a traditional full-length umbrella.

This is particularly important for our readers that live in "gun-unfriendly" states.

Ditto if you live in states like California, New York, and New Jersey where it's very difficult for mere mortals to get a carrying concealed weapon (CCW) permit.

And even if you are a concealed firearms permit holder, you should learn these valuable skills.

Why? You never know when circumstances might dictate that you cannot carry a pistol. (For example, when traveling to a state where your CCW permit is not valid, or when traveling overseas.)

An undercover cop recently told me why he and his colleagues love using canes, walking sticks and even umbrellas during any street combat scenario.

I was astonished at the number of effective moves available to the cane/stick fighter.

Range is the big advantage that canes have over blades and other impact weapons.

Striking and jabbing are still the premiere moves, easily done with nearly any style of cane.

Some follow-up moves and holds are more comfortably accomplished with a hooked cane than with a straight stick, but either style works just fine.

The real question is: What can I have in my possession most often that attracts the least attention?

The cane is a wonderful, low-profile, yet extremely effective fighting tool that most people can fit into their lives with a minimum of lifestyle disruption.

Most casual observers don't even notice when you have one with you and certainly don't believe them to represent a threat.

As for walking stick designs: From what I have heard and observed here in the U.S., if you are well dressed and groomed, then law enforcement officers in most jurisdictions will hardly give you a second glance if you are carrying a walking stick.

But if you are shabby looking and perceived as "riff-raff", then expect to get plenty of grief.

Canes, especially aluminum ones that look like true walking aids, are far less likely to attract suspicion than walking sticks.

I have an acquaintance who lives in Oakland, California who carries a dull silver aluminum cane with a big rubber tip.

This cane looks very unobtrusive if not downright innocuous. It is not until you pick it up that you realize that it has been retrofitted with a 1/2" steel rod firmly fastened into its hollow core. The phrase "the iron fist in the velvet glove" comes to mind!

I have another acquaintance that lives in a very rainy climate, near Seattle, Washington. He makes a habit of carrying a stout full length traditional umbrella whenever he gets out of his car.

Aside from misplacing several umbrellas over the years, he had no trouble. (And, by God's grace, he only needed to use it to protect himself from rain showers.)

Nearly all of the stick/cane fighting techniques apply to folded umbrellas, and they can also be used quite effectively for jabbing.

My general preference is to use a well-spaced two-handed grip in most situations, to maintain control and more importantly to assure retention of the stick.

This is akin to what has been taught for many years by police academies in the use of long ("riot") batons.

The last thing that you want to happen is to have Mr. Bad Guy gain control of your weapon. If that were to happen, you would become the "Owie" recipient instead of the "Owie" distributor!

Do some research on your local laws. In most jurisdictions, any blow with a striking weapon to the neck or head is considered potentially lethal.

Police academies emphasize this in their baton training ("Never strike above the chest unless you would draw your pistol and fire in the same circumstances").

So don't escalate to doing so unless you are absolutely confident that your life is threatened and you have no other choice.

It may sound sissified and a bit too prim and proper but most courts look at things in terms of equal force and a graduated response, roughly as follows:

If Mr. Bad guy uses his fists, then you can use your fists. If he uses a weapon, then you can use a weapon. If he strikes above the chest, then you can strike above the chest.

As a practical matter, there are no rules in trying to save your life in a street fight, but apparently there are in courthouses.

Yes, I realize that a graduated response is not realistic to expect, since street fights are fast and furious.

Most victims don't even recognize that their attacker is using a weapon until after the incident is over.

But again, a graduated response is what courts will expect in order to make a ruling of justifiable self-defense.

If you get into an absolutely lethal brawl (a truly "kill or be killed" situation) and you cannot disengage, by all means aim where you can do the most damage: The front or side of the neck.

The human neck is soft tissue, a bundle of nerves, veins, arteries, and windpipe. It is your surest target to end a fight quickly and decisively.

The same goes for hand-to-hand combat. Aim your punches at his throat.

But again, it is also the surest way to find yourself in a courtroom. I can't stress this enough: show discretion!

Resources

Here are some of our top selling books, including a New York Times bestseller, that will make perfect gifts for your loved ones…

The Patriot's Guide to (Legally) Hiding Your Guns From the Government... So They Don't Know They Exist and Can Never Confiscate Them

Get the book at **www.SpiesHideGuns.com**

The 7 Strategies of Hand-to-Hand Combat

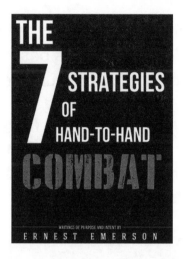

Get the book at **www.FreeSpyWarrior.com**

*Spy Secrets That Can Save Your Life (***New York Times Bestseller)*

Get the book at **www.FreeSecretBook.com**

The Escape Bag Blueprint: 37 Items You Must Have to Survive a Crisis.

Get the book at **www.Free37Secrets.com**

Spec Ops Power: How Elite Special Forces Commandos and Intelligence Operatives Stay Powered-Up On Top Secret Operations.

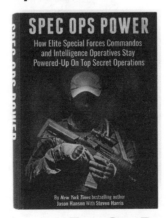

Get the book at **www.FreeSpyPower.com**

Bug Out Bag Guns: A Former CIA Officer's Treatise on the Guns (and Other Gear) You Need to Survive in a Hostile Environment.

Get the book at **www.FreeBugOutBook.com**

Survive Like a Spy: Real CIA Operatives Reveal How They Stay Safe in a Dangerous World and How You Can Too.

Get the book at **www.FreeCovertBook.com**

Alone and Unafraid: Patriot Defense and Survival Guide

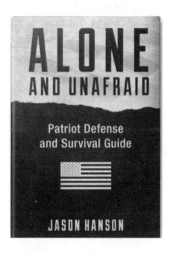

Get the book at **www.FreeWarriorBook.com**

The Little Black Book of 101 Spy Secrets

Get the book at **www.FreeSpyNow.com**

How to Build a Covert, Off the Grid Safe House Away from the Prying Eyes of the Government.

Get the book at **www.FreeCovertHouse.com**

Sleeper Cell Secrets of Spies and Our Founding Fathers

Get the book at
www.PatriotSleeperCell.com

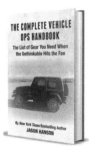

Survive a Shooting: Strategies to Survive Active Shooters and Terrorist Attacks

Get the book at **www.PatriotSniper.com**